THE FUNERAL

THE FUNERAL

A Pastor's Guide

John S. Mansell

ABINGDON PRESS
Nashville

THE FUNERAL
A PASTOR'S GUIDE

Copyright © 1998 by Abingdon Press

This book is printed on acid-free, recycled paper.

Library of Congress Cataloging-in-Publication Data

Mansell, John S.
    The funeral : a pastor's guide / John S. Mansell.
      p. cm.
    ISBN 0-687-06790-1 (pbk. : alk. paper)
    1. Funeral service. 2. Church work with the bereaved.
I. Title.
BV199.F8M36   1998
265'.85—dc21   98-21180
                                                  CIP

99 00 01 02 03 04 05 06 07—10 9 8 7 6 5 4 3 2

MANUFACTURED IN THE UNITED STATES OF AMERICA

To my spouse, Allene, for her editorial assistance
and pastoral presence during much of my shepherding.

To the cohorts who made all this "pawsible": Kitsie, Karma,
Socks, and Stormy, and in memory of J. B.

CONTENTS

CHAPTER ONE

The Phone Rings

I was rummaging through the cardboard boxes and drawers looking for the can opener. Two hungry cats loudly demanded to be fed—now. Then the phone rang. It was the funeral director on the other end of the line. I thought: "How did he get my number? We've been in town only a day." In a few short words, I learned that I had my first funeral to do in three days. With no idea where the can opener was and all our boxes still stacked to the ceiling, I quickly grabbed the church's pictorial directory and rushed out to visit with the family. (My spouse kindly volunteered to feed the cats.)

As I drove along beside tall green corn fields, I tried to compose myself. I told myself that I was a trained minister. I had graduated from a fine seminary and had the church's confidence behind me through the act of ordination. On one level, I was the expert going out to practice based on my expertise. On another level, unfortunately, I did not feel too confident in myself. Yes, I had been "proactive" by participating in special workshops on grief counseling and reflecting upon the theology of funerals; however, I had not received any nuts-and-bolts training in how to do a funeral. While I was fully prepared to deal with tears, I was not ready to offer prayers for the dead or offer a funeral sermon.

(Actually, I had yet to preach my first sermon at "my" first church.)

As with many aspects of ministry, when push came to shove, I stepped forward in faith. I unashamedly winged it. I guessed, improvised, and, when in doubt, had the family pray. When words failed, I prayed the Lord's Prayer. Those looking at me noted how calm, poised, and seasoned I was. In truth, I was a nervous wreck.

Following the experience, I promised myself I would get a clearer understanding of what resources a pastor needs at the time of a funeral. I studied various Protestant funeral service outlines and tried to figure out which made sense to me and why. I also reflected upon personal experiences in which I had lost a loved one and was in need of pastoral care. I noted that there were times when a pastor was especially comforting. On the other hand, I also shuddered as I recalled other occasions when a pastor was painfully ineffective. I realized that I needed a resource for how to conduct funeral services and ministry to the bereaved. This book is offered in part as the training manual I did not have when I started my ministry.

Getting Started

Each pastor has his or her own way of relating to pain, grief, and death. Think of a time when death touched your life. What happened and how did you process things? Did you stuff your feelings inside into an inner dark hole? Did you try to be the super caregiver who rescued everyone from their grief? Did you try to anesthetize the bereaved from their pain? Did you run around in a state of crisis barking out orders? Did you become unglued and melt away in a pool of tears? My point is not to judge which approach to death is right or wrong. As pastors, we are still mortals having to face perhaps the most difficult issue that can be dealt with: death. I encourage you to reflect upon your experiences so they will not complicate how you will be a pastor to your congregation.

I have learned that the first step in planning for the funeral service is pastoral care. By taking the example of the shepherd imagery in the Twenty-third Psalm, we see that our role is to lead. Bear in mind, however, that it is the bereaveds' responsibility to walk through the "valley of death." This may sound cruel and heartless. Clergy, as a whole, are a caring lot. They often feel the need to be heroic figures who can fix almost anything. While there are many things that clergy *can* do that express appropriate empathy in situations of grief, we are not God. We cannot give back to the bereaved what they ache for most—their departed loved one.

I invite you to think for a moment about what a shepherd does. Shepherds are not warm and fuzzy personalities seeking approval for being wonderful. Shepherds have a specific task: to care for the flock. Part of this task is to lead the sheep to still waters and green pastures. Another aspect of the shepherd's job description is to find lost sheep. While we may not think of it much, a shepherd is also called to defend the flock against harmful predators. Finally, a shepherd is required to care for any member of the flock that is in need—a mother lambing, a newborn, an injured sheep, or one in ill health. The shepherd does not say, "I feel your pain," and expect the flock to gush over the shepherd's charm. Instead, the shepherd deals with the specific needs of the flock. All these functions are required of a pastor during the time of a funeral.

As shepherds, clergy can help the family begin the grieving process, but we should never think of ourselves as the source or granter of healing. In fact, so much attention has been given to the grief process by the general media that

11

many of the bereaved come to me before the funeral and tell me they have worked through all the stages of grief.[1] At such times, the bereaved are still in the pre-stages of encountering their grief, and for that reason it does not help to challenge such sentiments directly. Your task is to stay focused and proceed with providing disciplined pastoral care. The degree of the bereaved's ability to resolve their grief issues is a mysterious one that goes beyond the scope of a funeral service.

But does that mean that a pastor should do nothing with regard to a family facing death? Heavens no! Be empathetic and intentional in your ministry to the family; however, do not have unrealistic expectation that there will be no more tears after the funeral service. What I try to do, instead, is encourage an intentional and integrated ministry of the whole church to the bereaved. I try to create safe and caring environments in which the bereaved have the opportunity to hear God's good news while confessing personal loss.

Of course, each church has a slightly different way of practicing the important ministry of caring for the bereaved. Oftentimes, a neighbor's steady shoulder is as effective—if not more so—in communicating Christian caring as any sermon preached from the pulpit. I try to work with the congregations I serve so that the many levels of the church function in a coordinated manner. For example, does the chair of the appropriate committee know the specific details and the needs for funerals as well as additional events? Does the secretary know who to contact, and when, to insure that all bases are covered? Does the sanctuary require special attention—for example, someone operating the sound system for the pastor and soloist(s) as well as staffing the tape recorder? (Personally, I think that videotaping a funeral service is inappropriate, and should be discouraged.) Has someone agreed to turn on the furnace or air conditioner, allowing the required time for climate control to be effective, or to clear the sidewalk of snow, ice, or leaves by a specified time? Part of being a good shepherd is being an effective administrator and diplomat. Appendix A at the end of the book provides a sample worklist as a guide for expediting this ministry.

Soon after I conducted my first funeral, I sat down and counted all the steps and people involved in conducting a effective funeral service. I was amazed! Many people and many duties are involved in a variety of complex sequential and parallel tasks. In fact, I have known churches that have been burnt out by funerals. To help deal with this "burden" or "chore" approach to funerals, I have developed a motivational/theological way at looking at the steps that lead to a funeral service. Everything that leads to a funeral, in some way or another, may be viewed as a liturgy to the bereaved. This liturgy has six parts to it: pastoral care; administration; diplomacy; chaplaincy to the family; leading worship; and communicating to the community.

Pastoral Care

When a clergyperson is notified of the death of a parishioner, two sets of general rules apply. (For special circumstances, see chapter 4 on pastoring when special conditions are involved.)

1. As soon as possible, contact the head of the family, express condolences (a brief prayer may be appropriate over the phone), and make arrangements that are mutually convenient for the purpose of pastoral care. Use some judgment here. If you are in the middle of a project that has to be done, like putting away the groceries or taking one's medicine, please take care of yourself first. The funeral marathon can often last from three to five days. Seldom is any attention

given to the pastor during this time. Don't expect anyone else to take care of you when you aren't willing to take care of yourself.

2. Upon arriving at the home of the bereaved, make as few assumptions as possible. Go into the home aware of what has just occurred. After initial remarks, listen carefully to determine the needs of the family and get a sense of their state of mind. Is a family member alone? Do you sense that someone else needs immediate medical attention? What urgent things were the family doing just prior to the death? Does one of the bereaved have to take medication? (I am thinking here of someone who might be diabetic or on heart or blood pressure medication.) Does a child need to be picked up or dropped off? How can you, as a pastor, be of assistance?

I liken such initial visits to providing triage care. An important underlying concern is to stabilize the bereaved as much as possible until additional assistance from other family members or neighbors arrives. As a general rule, I do not leave the bereaved alone if they are by themselves. I will ask the bereaved to have a family member or friend come over for emotional support. Often, I will ask a member of the church come over as well. I feel that it is important to spread out the stress of coping with the bereaved as much as possible. Just as a bridge can collapse under too much stress that is focused at one point for too long, so too can a pastor snap if he or she takes on too much of the coping demands for too long a period.

How does one conduct pastoral care to someone who has just lost a loved one? What should a clergyperson likely expect of the bereaved? I first thought that the circumstances around the death largely shaped the manner in which the bereaved experienced their grief. While such considerations do contribute to a degree when a person experiences loss, I have found that death is death. Regardless of the circumstances, death is painful. Put in another way, death is like a book that is given us. We open it and find the terrible words: "Your time has come. This is your journey through the dark valley. If you want to get out of the dark valley, you will have to cross through it." We may try to put our death book aside; however, it grabs us and demands that we read it.

I have found that when I arrive on the scene shortly after the family has learned of the death, the bereaved parishioner will likely repeat himself or herself countless times—expressing words of being overwhelmed as well as offering statements that suggest that nothing of importance has happened. Often, the bereaved may prefer to inquire about another person's sorrows. Regardless of what the bereaved say, listen attentively and patiently. Communicate a sense of permission for this sharing and listen empathetically to the bereaved; convey the fact that as a pastor you identify with their cross and consider it to be important to you.

Once the situation has stabilized, I give the bereaved my card so that we can talk later. Why do I do this? Don't the bereaved already have my phone number somewhere? The answer is yes, and that's the point—they have my phone number or address *somewhere*. Under the high stress of coping with death, small tasks suddenly become giant ones. By giving the bereaved family or individual my card and putting it next to the phone, I simplify their life when they try to contact me later. It is a small thing to do, but it is helpful to the family.

At this early point, don't talk about the pending funeral. The bereaved are not ready to process such a prospect. They are still looking backward, whereas planning for the funeral requires looking to the future. Try to give the family at least a day before approaching them on the subject of funeral preparations. Finally, you may want to make some general suggestions, such as that a family member stop by the grocery store to pick up some extra coffee and supplies. This suggestion may sound strange, but over and over again families have told me how much they appreciated this specific bit of advice. Sadly, in America today, families tend to gather together only at weddings and funerals. When a death happens, family members from the ends of the earth descend upon the primary family. By having extra supplies on hand (coffee, tea, sandwich ingredients, paper cups, tissues, paper towels, and *toilet paper),* some unfortunate events and words might be avoided. Depending upon the region of the country and the practices of the community, neighbors may drop by and leave consolation dishes for the family as well. These approaches to providing pastoral care to the bereaved hold also in situations in which a death vigil has been in effect at the home or in another setting.

Administration

All too often clergy are asked to conduct a funeral service for someone they do not know and who did not leave instructions with respect to their wishes for the service. When the family gathers with the pastor to plan the service, the family may have no idea what is needed to prepare a funeral sermon. Those families which have been actively connected to a faith community are probably familiar with the rituals of the funeral marathon. This experiential reference point can be of great assistance for the family. For those who do not have any frame of reference, either by faith or prior experiences of death in the family, this experience will be additionally difficult. Finally, families that have difficulty making decisions generally may likely have increased difficulty in making decisions during the time of a funeral.

When the family gathers with the pastor to plan the service, it generally has the expectation that, having just been with the funeral director who took care of the material aspects of the funeral service, the clergyperson will likewise "take care" of the spiritual matters of the funeral service. While the comparison is understandable from the viewpoint of the bereaved, I have found that it extends only so far. The tasks that the funeral director has to deal with, while many, are generally well defined. It may be helpful for clergypersons to observe funeral directors go through their procedure—from receiving and preparing a body to the lowering of the casket into the ground—to get a clearer sense of what is involved. However, in contrast, the clergyperson's duties relate primarily to the spiritual aspects of a funeral service and are thus, by definition, more open-ended. Although the family may expect to be able to have a clergy person "take care" of the arrangements, the spiritual realities require some special attention. While the funeral director's primary interest is for the dead, the pastor's concern is for the living.

When the family arrives to meet with the pastor, there are some simple things that can facilitate a more productive session. (Naturally, this process should be adapted as needed to fit your particular situation.)

Setting the Stage

Greet each individual personally. Make sure everyone is seated comfortably. Take wraps and offer coffee or tea. Have everyone introduce themselves to you as well as explain their relationship with the departed. Ask the family what their schedule is and how much time they have for the meeting. Offer your condolences and offer a *brief* prayer for the departed and for the purpose of the meeting. (This is optional, depending upon the family's openness to prayer.)

Data Collection

This is the time to work out specific details of the service, including the following:

Funeral schedule
Obituary information
Special needs

Ask if there are any special needs that the family might have at the service: perhaps mobility may be a concern; perhaps the congregation should be told *not* to wear perfume, cologne, or aftershave to the funeral service since some persons attending the service may have respiratory problems; or perhaps someone needs to plan on bringing an extra tank of oxygen for a family member.

Scripture and hymn selection
Music selection

Ask if there is anyone from the family who would want to say a few words about the departed during the funeral service or if there is a special reading that the family might have read.

Time of Remembering

This should be the bulk of the session. Ask the family to talk about some of their happy memories of the departed. I have found that the bereaved find it much easier to talk about something pleasant. As the family remembers the departed, don't encourage family of origin work! The bereaved will likely do this later as they go through the various stages of the grief process. Listen to how the bereaved talk. I have often noted that family members revisit memories that are long past and humorously relive the experience. I pay special attention to body language, changes in vocal quality, tonality, and pauses, to help me discern the significance of a particular statement. As I listen attentively, I try to gather as many metaphors as possible that the family associate with the departed—either directly or indirectly. Usually, I will gently ask others to speak. While I do this to get as much information as possible for the purposes of the funeral sermon, I am also mindful that giving voice to someone is a powerful way of establishing rapport as well as inclusion. When I ask someone something, I am communicating that I take that person seriously and that they have something of great significance to offer.

When the family members have finished sharing, I will paraphrase what has been said thus far, which will often facilitate further comments. I will then briefly summarize all that I have heard to show the family my mental sketch of the departed, which will again likely produce additional comments. After I have clarified with the family my understanding of the departed's life, I will briefly summarize the particulars discussed regarding the entire service as well as specific task assignments and timelines. Finally, I will walk the family through the day of the service—not only to make sure that everyone knows the schedule and place of events, but also to gently prepare them for what is to come—one of the most trying moments for the family to face. If bad weather will be a factor, I will ask the family to prepare for it and plan on wearing the necessary clothing for the committal service.[2]

Closing and Benediction

At this point, I will usually offer remarks of sympathy and goodwill for the family. Oftentimes, I will have the family close with the Lord's Prayer. After this, the family leaves—taking their things and disposing of tissues as they go. As I say goodbye, I again make sure to shake everyone's hand.

19

Self-care and Separation

Once I close the door of the pastor's office, I take a few deep breaths and let them go slowly. I pause and allow my mind to clear. When I return to my desk, I go over the funeral service file I have made. (The file should have the name of the departed on it as well as the date and time of the funeral service. It does not reflect well upon a pastor to forget a funeral. Amazingly, it happens all too often!) When I review the file, I jot down things on a "to do" list and attach it to the top outside cover of the file. If any phone calls need to be made, I make them at this time. Finally, when I put the phone down, I get up and go for a walk. It is important for a clergyperson not to become engulfed by the emotional distress of the family.

Diplomacy

I have talked at length about the administrative aspects of the funeral planning session. I want to focus now on the diplomatic side of this liturgy to the bereaved. I have noticed that death is like brewing tea. All the emotions begin boiling and create a brew that is often quite unexpected. Normal, well-behaved adults, upon feeling the impact of death, may behave in ways that would be unthinkable beforehand. On the other hand, I have seen feuding families suspend their quarrels (temporarily) out of respect for the dead. Unfortunately, although a minister cannot impose civility upon a family that is determined to be uncivil, there are a number of things that clergy can do to increase the likelihood of family cooperation. I find that the liturgy of diplomacy can be broken down into the following steps: awareness; inclusion; and clarification and framing of common concerns.

Awareness

When the family comes to the office (or when I go out to visit the family at their home or other agreed-upon location), I pay special attention to how the family members situate themselves and relate to one another. This arrangement of the family can be meaningful, for it provides needed clues to understand the family and the life of the departed in a deeper way. Family members will often group themselves in smaller clusters with noticeable gaps between other groupings. This may signal that there are underlying tensions separating these groups. One way I deal with this is to have everyone sit in one circle. Another kind of situation occurs when family members sit in a circle around another family member as if they are in "orbit" around that family member. The "orbiting" family members may often fall over themselves trying to prove themselves to the "orbited" family member. If this should start happening, remarks made could get rather "unfortunate" very quickly—with the words being remembered for generations. This is particularly the case if the "orbited" family member is not the primarily related bereaved family member—such as a spouse. The "governing" aunt, uncle, patriarch, or matriarch can create havoc by trying to impose his or her "proper" advice. Again, by structuring how people sit, and by guiding the discussion, the pastor can reduce the likelihood of this unfortunate family scripting.

Inclusion

This discussion leads me to some reflections about how clergypersons should present themselves to the bereaved, as well as how the bereaved often present themselves to the pastor.[3] How you present yourself is critical for facilitating a sense of inclusion in a group. Those who have participated in CPE training will be familiar with attentive listening techniques, active listening skills, and focusing strategies that can enhance discussion.[4] As the clergyperson relates to the bereaved, it is important to be intentional, follow a game plan, adapt as needed, and model a Christian presence.

When a person comes to a pastor, we must remember who is "professionally" in need and who is in control. While we may all have personal needs, those who, by way of their profession, are authorized to deal with people's personal needs must not mix their own needs with attending to the needs of others. By definition, the bereaved family is in need and not in control of their actions as they normally would be. Conversely, the clergyperson is not immediately bereaved and is obligated to be in control of his or her actions and words so that no further pain is inflicted upon the bereaved family.[5] Again, it is crucial for the clergyperson to be intentionally in control of himself or herself. This is a reminder that a clergyperson is obligated to conduct himself or herself with uncompromising fidelity. As a shepherd cares for a wounded lamb but does not become emotionally emmeshed in the psychological processes of the lamb, so too a clergyperson must be empathetic but self-controlled while conducting the session with the bereaved.

When death strikes a family, the spiritual portrait of the family is significantly impacted. I visualize it this way. A family is like a large quilt. When someone in a family dies, a large hole is cut into the quilt. It is the task of the bereaved to weave a new pattern into the quilt so that the quilt is repaired. This requires pain and tears. All of the family members, in some way or another, will take part in this effort. Some of the family members will be heroes, while others will play the role of the family black sheep. The pastor, as a shepherd, can model structure, continuity, inclusion, empathy, and impartiality for each of the family members, as well as be confessional in acknowledging the loss to facilitate this grief work process.[6] By following the administrative tasks for the funeral planning session discussed above, the very needs for structure, continuity, and inclusion may become the balm that leads to grace. By engaging the family in prayer, the family will experience a communal recognition of the death. This is an important additional step of the journey through the dark valley.

Clarification and Framing of Common Concerns

How many times have we heard a family member say: "I'm the *only* one experiencing pain. All the rest don't care!" After making such a statement, that particular person may often storm away with a dark cloud over his or her head and leave the remaining family members treading water in the sea of guilt poured on them.

When someone dies, there is not one grief but many. All the family members are experiencing the loss in ways unique to themselves. While there may be a common presentation of the family's bereavement, there likely is a very diverse, individual experience of this loss. By following the steps described above regarding inclusion, the deeply personal feelings of loss held by each of the bereaved family members are honored as much as possible in the framing of their common concern.

I remember one family that was very divided over planning the funeral service for "Martha"—sister, wife, mother, aunt, and grandmother. One group wanted to be loyal to Martha and remember her with a degree of respect that defied reality. Another group was disappointed that Martha had not accomplished more in her life. The tension in the pastor's office grew as the "loyal" group felt that the "disappointed" group was not taking their viewpoint seriously. (It is quite common for feelings of abandonment to surface during the time of the funeral.) Finally, after much effort, I was able to find one particular quality which both sides agreed upon that appropriately described Martha: her love of fishing. One family member said: "You know, I had forgotten all about that. It's perfect." Laughter soon replaced the tension as the family realized they did have a common concern with respect to Martha. While Martha's death was painful, at least the remaining family members drew comfort from being able to pull together and remember her in a fitting way—a small success that should not be trivialized.

Chaplaincy to the Bereaved

I have been part of and served churches in the West and Midwest and have found that, despite the marked geographic and cultural differences between these regions, a clergyperson is a chaplain to the bereaved family regardless of location. When the family gathers to remember the departed, there is a need for both community acknowledgment and family confidentiality and privacy. I want to consider privacy now and reserve my remarks regarding community acknowledgment for later in my discussion about the liturgy of communicating to the community.

Based upon observation, the last thing a bereaved family—or any family—wants is public embarrassment. The death of a loved one often makes a family feel very vulnerable to public scrutiny. They do not want their grief "exposed" or "compared" to another family's grief for fear it might result in the invalidation of their own experience of grief. To meet this need for privacy, faith communities have developed various ways by which a family remembers the dead apart from the community remembrance of the departed. Here, a clergyperson can play an active role in facilitating these private observances.

Generally speaking, I have found that faith communities employ two types of private observances for the departed: family viewing and eulogizing. The former, understandably, can be very difficult. I remember that when my grandmother passed away, my family was embarrassed because they felt they did not know how to conduct themselves "properly" at the time of viewing. There were quite a few needless words said over what was right and wrong. While such concerns seem silly, they point to the deeper difficulty of viewing the corpse of the departed together as a family. The appearance of the corpse may well be significantly different from what the family remembers about the departed, which can be quite unsettling for the family. Conversely, the family members may be unable to see any difference at all. Often, I have been with widows or widowers who say that their spouse still looks like he or she did when they were first married—as if time had not passed. Regardless of how the bereaved experience this difference, it is important for a viewing to occur. The rationale for viewing the body (if it is at all possible) is to bring additional confirmation of the death, as well as provide moments of closure for the bereaved.

I have often been asked to lead the family during this time with a short service and a prayer, as well as walk with the bereaved as they view the body. When one stops over a casket and beholds the departed, one may be profoundly affected. One may sense time stop as one processes the experience. On one occasion, I observed a very successful career woman who was approaching her mother's casket. While the death was no surprise, the reality of confronting the death and acknowledging the fact that an entire generation of family was now gone was overwhelming. She gently grabbed hold of the tiny hand of a grandchild and began to explain to the grandchild what they were doing, what was going on, who had died, and what that all meant. She told the tiny child to be strong and not to worry. I then noticed that the grandmother positioned the child between herself and the casket. In a very unsophisticated way, this very sophisticated woman was talking out her grief via the tiny child. The rest of the family saw this but said nothing. They were allowing this woman a moment of privacy amidst the greater family presence. A clergyperson can be of great comfort at this particular time by providing answers that are timely, clear, and understandable, or by honoring moments of tears or silences. Most important, though, is a clergyperson's empathetic presence, which may be that needed staff the family needs to lean on to keep their footing.

Sometimes during this observance, the family will indicate its appreciation for the pastor's presence but express a desire to be alone. At that time, I may ask the family to form a circle, hold hands, and pray the Lord's Prayer together.[7] Finally, before I leave, I will double check with the family about the funeral schedule and the anticipated arrival times of other family members.

The second kind of private observance is that of eulogizing or remembering. During this kind of service, a clergyperson is asked to give a few opening remarks and then facilitate the family sharing of anecdotal accounts about the departed. At this time, family members may share poems that the departed was fond of or offer words that describe the meaning or quality of the relationship he or she had with the departed.[8] While some churches make this very complicated, I have found that simplicity is helpful.

"Clifford's" family had asked me to help them lead a brief service of remembrance for Clifford; it was the expected thing to do. About forty-five minutes before the funeral service, I invited the family up from the basement fellowship hall and brought them to the fireside room. I had them bring up chairs from the fellowship hall so that everyone would have a place to sit. (Sometimes, the custodian forgets or the requested task simply doesn't get done.) To be honest, I was glad that the custodian had not set up the chairs; this was an active family with a great deal of energy. In particular, the men in the family needed to do something. By bringing the chairs up to the fireside room, they were able to release some of their tension.

As I began to lead the family in this private service, I quickly realized they didn't feel comfortable about it. Since most of the older family members had meager educational backgrounds, they were painfully self-conscious and afraid of saying anything that might be taken as "downright stupid or embarrassing" (the fear they expressed). With strange blank expressions on the faces of the gathered family and the clock ticking, I started with prayer and paraphrased Clifford's obituary to set the context for the family to offer their experiences. At each major shift or stage in his life, I paused and rephrased that stage in an open-ended way. As I did this, family members began sharing their "expertise"—their knowledge of Clifford.

When one person stopped talking, I asked another open-ended question that facilitated another response. As the family became comfortable with this pattern, they initiated their own sharing. While there were the expected tears, there were also humorous accounts that led everyone to laughter. When appropriate, I inserted a timely (and brief) pastoral comment or two and directed the flow of the sharing, as there was only a limited amount of time for this private service. Everyone had a chance to share something—most, in fact, did. Finally, the funeral director cued me to close the time so the family could prepare for the actual funeral service. After the funeral, family members thanked me especially for helping them remember Clifford in such a caring, informal, and yet spiritual way. They confessed that they did not know how to do a eulogy service, were afraid of public speaking, and greatly appreciated my tactful guidance which permitted them to learn as they went.

Some faith communities hold both observances by scheduling the family viewing for the night before the funeral and the eulogizing just before the funeral service. I cannot emphasize enough how important it is for a clergyperson to become aware of the local funeral traditions of their community—not only regarding words used but content and expectations as well.

Leading Worship

Oddly enough, like a wedding ceremony, the funeral service is also a time when pledges and promises are squared with reality. For the bereaved family as well as the clergyperson, the funeral service can be a deeply uplifting experience; however, it also can leave everyone in the pits of depression.

While there is no magic formula that will guarantee a perfect funeral service, I have found that organization and attention to detail ahead of time increase the likelihood that the service will be effective.

Well before the anticipated arrival of the funeral party, I conduct a walk through of the sanctuary and the church to make certain that everything is ready. I will often greet the women of the church who are preparing the coffee or consolation dishes and check to see how things are going. Next, I put the sermon folder (with sermon inside!) on the pulpit; set up the Bible for the selected reading(s); distribute service outlines to the funeral director, organist, and soloist(s); and have a glass of water put on the pulpit. Depending upon the church, the sound system may need to be turned on in advance. About this time, I will meet briefly with the funeral director about scheduling—getting our signals straight, reviewing service choreography, and synchronizing our watches. I will huddle similarly with the organist and soloist(s). Finally, I will return to my office and fill out the pastor's consolation card so that it can be given to the family after the services are over. After I have reviewed my checklist and have prepared myself for worship, I am ready to be with the family of the departed.

Each family behaves differently before a funeral. Often there will be a period of introductions of family members who have never met. If I could generalize at all, the family will behave the way it usually does at a family gathering (such as Thanksgiving or Christmas) but even more so. Thus, a clergyperson needs to be both a diplomat and a vigilant shepherd while remaining focused on the events that are about to take place. A clergyperson must not spend so much attention to caring for the family that he or she is not fully prepared to lead the worship service. A clergyperson's empathetic composure can be an anchor for the family.

Communicating to the Community

Several years ago, I was visiting with a funeral director after a huge funeral. There were cars parked everywhere—even in the snow-covered soybean fields. The funeral director reflected that the day before he had been the only one present at a homeless person's funeral. While the importance of both deaths was the same in God's eyes, evidently the community perceived the two deaths differently. Another time, an elderly woman—who had been a longtime member of the church and had also outlived all of her family and friends—was buried and I was the only church representative present. I thought of the many funerals she must have attended, while now she was laid to rest alone. I can imagine few things worse than one's death not being recognized by one's community. This need for recognition of the departed is one reason the AIDS Names Quilts have taken on such significance in the ongoing fight against this dreadful disease.

We live in a very complex and fragmented world. Death either presents us with an occasion to escalate this sense of disconnection, or provides us with the opportunity for grace by restoring some degree of wholeness to our lives. In his poem "Departmental," Robert Frost confronts us with our tendency to dehumanize one another through the many rituals that govern our lives. Ironically, Frost uses the unlikely protagonist of an ant to expose our highly civilized bias towards seeing the experiences of others—even in the case of death—as insignificant and beyond the scope of personal reflection.

Frost suggests that in order to maintain social order and the proper function of society, we separate from one another lest we become compromised or contaminated by another's joy or sorrow. Through the burial process of an ant, Frost depicts our own reluctance to take the time to pause from our busy lives in order to become more aware of another sojourner in life. Despite our tendency to hide behind our many appearances of honor, public decrees, and solemn pageantry, Frost challenges us to confess the often frightening nature of our own existence. He speaks of an ant who, while hurrying unaware across the body of one of its species,

> Isn't given a moment's arrest—
> Seems not even impressed[9]

Ours is the task to step forward in faith and, in grace-filled ways, weave solitary figures together into a community of faith as they indeed risk the pain of confronting separation while recalling deeply felt memories of the departed.

Depending on the circumstances, the clergyperson may be the first to know of the death or may learn of it by way of a church member. Regardless of the situation, it is important that the faith community be informed of the death and funeral arrangements in an orderly manner. In small communities, word of mouth will provide the initial report of the death. The notice in the worship bulletin or newsletter or a publicly recognized location, such as at the post office or a florist's shop, will serve more as a ceremonial recognition of the death. In larger communities, where people do not know each other, some kind of telephone-tree/prayer-line is very helpful. While published obituaries provide a good deal of information, there is no substitute for the personal contact of a caring church member.

Death confronts us with ambiguity. The community, on some level, is aware of this. I have found that giving clear, timely, and understandable instructions and guidance to the community before, during, and after the service(s) comforts the community. This is especially the case regarding all the little details that pertain to a funeral, even though these sundry details will vary from church to church.

While I am reluctant to spend too much time on the subject, a clergyperson should also model civility to the community. People will be people. One of the temptations before, during, and after a funeral is for the congregation to gossip. This is not helpful for the bereaved or the congregation. While such practices may fill in the holes for the curious regarding the departed, gossip is often wrong, hurtful, and ultimately based on a selfish desire to be in control. I remember one death in particular which the community attributed to all sorts of immoral behavior when, in fact, the departed had simply died of natural causes. Finally, during

31

the funeral service, a clergyperson can grant permission to the grieving to process their grief in particularly appropriate ways.

Closing Thoughts

In the sections that follow, I have provided sample sermons and reflections that introduce each sermon. At the end of this work, I have provided appendices to help the reader integrate my thoughts into his or her pastoral ministry. For the seminarian preparing for pastoral service, I hope these words serve as guideposts—albeit fallible—as you minister to people in perhaps the darkest moments of their lives.

If I could offer one final word of advice: listen. Saint Francis of Assisi was so right when he wrote: "it is better to understand than to be understood..." Ultimately, the mystery of death may be revealed through God's grace. By providing attentive ears, courage, resolve, and hope, we, as clergy, assist the bereaved as they conduct their pilgrimage through the dark valley. The apostle Paul wrote so accurately about the "sting of death." We must *never* trivialize the wounds of the soul that death brings; however, we must always remember that the tomb was found empty. We are an Easter-oriented people. Ultimately, we live by this hope.

The night before I was to take my Pauline Greek final in seminary, I learned that a beloved professor had died unexpectedly. When I thought of this professor and how he seemed to be such an incarnation of life, death seemed to be a logical incongruity to his nature. I found myself overwhelmed with feelings of loss, as he had been the father-figure I had not had earlier in my life. He had taught New Testament and had specialized in the letters of Paul. I remember putting down the phone receiver after hearing the news of his death, feeling numb all over. When I took that Greek final the next day, I was not in a particularly good frame of mind. While I thought my deceased professor would have been proud of the progress I had made, I felt as though I was treading water. I was nearly done with the final. I knew I was doing well. And then it hit! I came to the last question; I was to translate, without aid of a dictionary, a long passage from Paul. A voice from within pleaded that the passage not be on death; however, I immediately recognized Paul's teachings from 1 Corinthians 15. Each word seemed to burn within me. The pain of life without this professor seemed too great. Part of me wanted to give up and stop. However, a deeper voice commanded me to move forward in spite of my anguish.

As I translated the passage, it was as if each word was taunting me. I raged inside at the unfairness of death. There would be no opportunities for words of caring and appreciation to be said. It was over, and I could not turn off the pain. It was not until later, at his funeral service, that I was able to cry tears like a flooding river and felt the healing release promised in that passage by Paul.

I wish you peace in your ministry, a rod and staff to keep you balanced, and plenty of tissues for the tears along the way.

CHAPTER TWO

Preparing for the Funeral Sermon

Sermon writing is difficult and paradoxically easy—both at the same time. In the sermon message, one is wrestling often with the most painful and disturbing aspects of life. To take such a journey on a regular basis requires integrity, a disciplined openness to the work of the Spirit, and a deep yearning to answer and live out one's calling to follow in the footsteps of Christ. When one enters into such reflection, one is forced to confront one's own limits, deficits, and shortcomings. Often, it is much easier to take shortcuts and settle for the generic; however, this is not the way of the Spirit.

Conversely, when one does set aside one's own agendas, self-talk, and illusions, and becomes immersed in the unfolding drama of salvation, moments of epiphany may explode into one's consciousness so often that human speech scarcely has the ability to render justice to the experience. It is my firm conviction that sermon composition is often this way—the fingers or the hand racing to capture or depict the glory and inspiration of that moment of epiphany.

I will not try to tell another person how to compose or deliver a sermon, as there are already many experts whose wisdom is readily available. Writing aspects aside, however, sermon composition is—in part—a mysterious process that is ultimately based upon one's relationship with God that is discerned through prayer, disciplined reading of the text, and the genuine relationships that one has in the community of believers. "Schtick" rings hollow. All this is to say that a funeral sermon must be crafted with spiritual and intellectual integrity. One must not go the way of saying something that one knows is not the case. Why is this? For me, the answer is simple. We, as clergypersons, have been given a priceless gift—the calling from God to serve God's people. This is our ultimate foundation. The degree to which we play loose with this gift also weakens our foundation. At some point, if our words and deeds are not built upon our one foundation, then our efforts will be exposed for what they really are: vanity. This is not the cause of Christ!

Starting Points

These thoughts reflect the thinking and experience of one who works within the "Beltway" of Christianity, and are the sort you would expect to encounter in the seminary, the judicatory headquarters, or the church office. Now let me share something from another perspective. I was riding in the front seat of a hearse heading toward the cemetery. There had been a series of exceptionally difficult funerals in a short period of time. The funeral director and I were both aware of the strain that we were operating under. (Remember, funeral directors are people too!) He said: "I appreciated your message today, but in a way that may surprise you. Your content was fine; however, you seemed to give your message as if you were talking about someone who was very close to you. You seem to be able to get into the shoes of the departed as well as the bereaved. You did something else. You kept your words to a minimum. With all the pain that the bereaved are experiencing, time does funny things. To the grieving family, a five-minute message seems like a ten- or fifteen-minute message. You showed great respect for the grieving by presenting your remarks in the way that you did."

I was surprised by these words of advice because the funeral director came from a faith tradition that prided itself on half-hour sermons; however, the more I reflected upon his words, the more they seemed appropriate.

The funeral sermon is a time when the faith community weaves fitting words of faith around the life of the departed. During the funeral sermon, the life of the departed is remembered in ways that authentically convey Christian caring and respect for the bereaved, as well as rehearse to the listeners their own finitude within the context of God's unfolding infinity.

I use a benchmark phrase to determine if my funeral message is on track. I ask myself: "Am I doing right by the departed?" If the answer is yes, then I proceed. If the answer is no, then I have to take a hard look at myself. I remember a funeral service performed by a neighboring pastor. The whole town was in attendance. At the end of the service, the townfolk left shaking their heads saying: "That preacher sure didn't do right by Elmer."

So then, how do we "do right" by the departed? Let me suggest that you begin by using the information gathered in the funeral planning session as a reference point in your message. Next, draw upon whatever personal experiences you may have had with the departed. Search for a phrase that shows how the departed lived life. (Some discretion should be used in order to refrain from communicating uncivil remarks.[1]) Focus chiefly on how the departed lived life—not on the causes of the person's death. Finally, after you have done what you can, quiet yourself and let God speak. If you need additional help, go for a walk, work in the garden, go for a drive, or do whatever you do that opens you up to the creative energy of the Spirit.

A Thorny Issue

Before we move on to offering more specific ideas for preparing funeral sermons, some attention to the thorny issue of clergy remuneration for pastoral services rendered on behalf of both the departed and the bereaved is in order. Depending on the polity of the denomination of which you are a member, you should use the initial negotiations with a congregation in view of a call, or the early days of a new pastoral appointment, to clarify the church's remuneration policy with respect to funerals. Each church is different. Make no assumptions that you and your new community of faith are somehow on the same wavelength on this issue. The failure to clarify such matters early on almost always leads to trouble down the road.

With these central words of warning in mind, let me offer some general remarks about clergy funeral remuneration that will apply in most instances. There is a typical understanding that clergy are not "paid" for performing the funeral service of church members, while a designated fee is usually set for non-church members. At the same time, bear in mind that the family of the departed church member is often encouraged to "do right" by the pastor by surprising the pastor with a gift. I remember that when my grandmother died, the moderator of the church pulled me aside the following Sunday and informed me precisely how I was to "surprise" my pastor. He said that a funeral service was over-and-beyond normal pastoral duties, and therefore it was the decent thing to do to remember the pastor with a gift; he even told me a very specific dollar amount for the gift. No one insisted that I had to give the "surprise" to my pastor; however, I would not have been able to hold my head up with any degree of respect within that church if I had not honored this caring custom.[2]

Space does not permit me here a thorough discussion of the historical practices of pastoral remuneration in exchange for officiating at a funeral; however, this is an increasingly important issue for the following reasons: (1) as funeral costs approach $10,000, a fair expression by the family to the clergy is in order; (2) as clergy compensation packages fall ever-increasingly behind the cost of living, the need for remuneration increases dramatically; and (3) many of the historical practices that precluded families from reimbursing a clergyperson for his or her efforts are no longer in effect.

This is to say that it is critical for a clergyperson and the governing board of the church to come to an official understanding regarding funeral reimbursement, and that this understanding be duly recorded in the official minutes of the church. This decision should be communicated to the congregation just as other items of church business are "officially" made public. A clergyperson may also want to visit the local funeral director to educate the funeral director regarding the church's policy pertaining to funeral remuneration. While this may sound like a lot of needless work, by doing so in advance, you may prevent a great deal of heartache down the road.

CHAPTER THREE

Sample Funeral Sermons

This chapter provides sample sermons as well as reflections on each. I invite you to consider these offerings as representatives of specific funeral situations. As you read each, ask yourself how you would craft a sermon in this situation. Try to think of other situations in which you would be called to perform the funeral, and reflect similarly on how you would minister to the bereaved through the funeral sermon.

A Healer's Paradox

Bill was sick—so ill that he lay near death. It seemed so odd. He had been a healer in the community most of his entire adult life. He had enjoyed life and was an evangelist for seizing the day. Now a strange disease was ravaging Bill's body. The doctors tried their best. Tubes were placed everywhere in Bill's body—tubes inside of tubes. I thought a plumber must have configured and installed such a complicated system of pipes and drains. He needed a respirator to breathe for him. The hums, buzzes, and beeps of the machines that kept him alive were deafening.

Bill was such a kind man. Now, as his body was being conquered by a disease medical researchers were not sure they even had a name for, Bill had questions. As he lay in his

41

hospital bed, he wanted to know why: Why, in the prime of his life should his life be taken away from him by inches? What had he done to justify such untreatable pain? What would happen to his wife and family when he was no longer there for them? Why? Why? Why?

I visited with him daily. If any person personified health and wholeness, it was Bill before his illness. While he had saved so many lives, nothing could be done to save him. I tried not to notice how his body was wasting way before my very eyes. I did not know a body could deteriorate that quickly. While it takes nine months for a fetus to become fully formed and ready to start its new chapter in life, Bill's rapid deterioration was occurring in a few short weeks.

On a very deep level, Bill knew what was happening to him. We privately shared from the deepness of such awarenesses. One afternoon, shortly after we finished visiting, Bill's heart monitor blared, and the blip on the screen went flat. Bill was dead.

❖   ❖   ❖

For a Healer
(Based on Psalm 121)

We are here today to celebrate the life of Bill—a special person who played an important role in many lives and who will be sorely missed. As I look out among you, I can see that Bill did, in fact, touch many lives. While he never thought that he did anything out of the ordinary, we all know otherwise.

As a healer, Bill helped many of us get well. If we had any questions, he would explain everything to us patiently. If there were worries weighing heavily upon us, he would take the time to listen and offer sensitive advice. Bill put principles first. His goal was to help people get well. No one was ever denied needed medical care because of insufficient funds.

Bill was also a person of keen intellect and faith. Trained in the scientific method, Bill's mind was always trying to understand better the universe we live in. This disciplined pursuit of truth included his faith. As I spoke with him over the course of these past months as he came to terms with his illness, I was moved by the strength of his faith. As we prayed, laughed, and cried together, I found myself inspired by his never compromising courage and devotion to God.

Bill was also a faithful spouse. We all hope that love grows in a marriage. In the case of Bill and June, as his health continued to decline, their love for each other blossomed even more. As I share this message with you, I wish I could give some clear-cut reason why Bill and June had to suffer so, but I cannot. I cannot explain why suffering exists in a universe created by a loving God. Neither can I explain the necessity of the cross. But the same God who loved the world enough to give us Jesus also knows our pains and sorrows before we are aware of them. In times such as these, we shed not only our tears, but God's as well.

Through the tears, we must say goodbye. It is hard to do this. I can't go past Bill's office without imagining Bill's smiling face. But we must say goodbye to Bill. And we must keep hold of the many wonderful memories we have of him. We can celebrate the gift of life that touched so many so deeply. We can rejoice that Bill's life was one full of happiness more often than sadness, and health more than sickness, and that he is no longer suffering. After living a life of service to others, Bill was moved to learn that all the churches in the community were praying for him. It is a humbling event in one's life to have hundreds, if not thousands, of people praying for you. Those prayers meant a lot to Bill. Those prayers, he said, helped him keep going.

Bill is now at peace. He has fought the good fight and run the race to the finish line. Now God has welcomed Bill into a new heavenly home. We can be comforted and at peace even in our grief, because we know Bill is at peace. We know that Bill rests in God's protection and care. We know that

> He will not let your foot be moved;
> he who keeps you will not slumber.
> He who keeps Israel
> will neither slumber nor sleep.
> The LORD is your keeper;
> the LORD is your shade at your right hand.
> The sun shall not strike you by day,
> nor the moon by night. (Psalm 121:3-6).

Jesus made the same promise when he reassured his disciples by saying: "Peace I leave with you; my peace I give to you. I do not give to you as the world gives. Do not let your hearts be troubled, and do not let them be afraid." (John 14:27).

Friends, let us rejoice in the life of Bill and know that he is at peace. AMEN.

❖   ❖   ❖

The Gift of a Teacher

Gail's health was failing. Actually, it had been failing for the last twenty years. People were used to seeing her slip into and out of critical condition. That pattern, however, would not be the case this time. As a teacher, Gail taught several generations of children to climb up to higher vistas; now she lay dying—and, sadly, her body wouldn't release itself to its final rest. For weeks Gail hung between life and death. Her breathing resembled that of an old steam locomotive straining to climb up a steep mountain grade. There was nothing that could be done to reverse the tide of so many years—and still she strained.

A family member asked me if it would be a sin just to let her go—when to take additional heroic measures would merely prolong her suffering. I looked into the family member's eyes and added my deep sobs to hers. I said: "No, it would be no sin. The doctors have done all that they can. At some point, we all have to die." And yet the decision was hard to make. To give up a loved one is a very difficult thing to do. Gail loved life deeply. She bravely fought the good fight for four additional days—experiencing degrees of prolonged suffering that I have never witnessed before or since.

❖   ❖   ❖

On Eagles' Wings
(Based on Psalm 91)

The Ninety-first Psalm speaks wonderfully of the nurturing relationship that God has with us. Taking a cue from nature, the psalmist uses the image of the parent eagle teaching the eaglet how to fly. The parent eagle does this by soaring high into the sky with the eaglet under its wings; when the eagle gets to a certain height, the eagle lets the eaglet go. As the eaglet falls, it has an opportunity to find its wings and learn how to fly; however, the parent eagle doesn't abandon its child. If the parent senses that the eaglet is having difficulty, then the mighty bird swiftly descends and gently catches the falling little one with its powerful pinions. Underneath the protective shelter of the parent eagle's wings, the eaglet is carried to safety—ready for another lesson.

When I think of this passage, I think of Gail. Just as the psalmist talks about how God prepares us for life, Gail prepared many for their journeys in life. As a teacher, Gail thoughtfully touched many lives. She sought passionately to instill in her students not only the needed knowledge but also the sense of direction that was required to face life's challenges.

Her smile revealed a tempered joy for life. Her faith provided strength for others in times of need. Her sense of urgency captured her students' attention and helped them realize that what they were about was important. Throughout all this, Gail was gracious, loving, patient, fun-loving, yet persistent in her calling in life. Gail had a strong sense of duty. She felt it was important to care for those in need.

As we say goodbye to Gail today and express our appreciation for her life, let us feel free to treasure the special and unique ways Gail touched our lives. Gail was a special person—gentle, warm, and caring. It is a tribute to her love for life that she had so many friends. Cherish these memories. Help one another hold dear these special moments; however, let Gail go to her final resting place in peace.

When we gather to say goodbye to a loved one, we bear a double wound. The first is the actual passing of our beloved. The second is the pain we bear in our hearts. Friends, even amidst the darkness of death, there is good news and hope. God ministers to both our wounds; God has a way of using our tears to heal our hearts. Over time, we will come to see Gail as being with her Lord, for our Lord, like the parent eagle, has already delivered Gail from harm. Under the wings of God Almighty, Gail has found a safe refuge, a protective fortress, and a calming shade.

Gail knew her God. Now her God has called to her by name. There will be no more fear by night or dread over the arrows that fly by day. Our God has called her home and has honored her with eternal rest. Gail has been raised up on eagle's wings to begin her new tomorrow. AMEN.

❖   ❖   ❖

Waiting for Sunset

Beth was nearly one hundred years old. She had been in the care center for quite some time. I visited her weekly. Her once-strong body now resembled the shriveled up stocks of corn that she used to pass by when she walked. She could not speak—a stroke had taken that pleasure from her several years ago. When I visited her, I would hold her hand. She would smile as much as she could. I would tell her of the goings-on at the church, update her about the youth activities, and always close our visits with a prayer.

On one particular visit, I noticed that she looked especially frail. I told her I would be away for a few days as I had a church meeting to attend. When I left, I did not think I would ever see her alive again. The following week passed quickly; I was involved in the nonstop meetings that are part and parcel of such church gatherings.

When I returned, I was surprised by a phone call from the care center. The nurse asked me to come over as Beth was near death. Somehow, Beth had summoned the needed strength to hold on until I returned. I quickly went over to the care center and sat beside Beth. I gently held her hand as I had so many times before, but this time I began praying last prayers. I could tell she recognized me by the movement of her eyes. I said goodbye to her and was humbled by the fact that this woman cared so much for me that she would wait until my return before making the final journey.

❖   ❖   ❖

A Room in God's House
(Based on John 14)

We gather today to be reminded of God's promises to us as we honor the life of Beth and mourn her passing as family members or friends.

When someone we love dies, we long to feel God's comforting presence; yet, in this time of great need, we may feel that God is distant and remote, or that somehow our prayers are not heard. We may find that it is difficult to collect our emotions and try to pray at all. At such times we may find comfort and reassurance in the promises Jesus makes to his disciples. The promises Jesus makes in John 14 are simple words, but the message conveys so much. Jesus speaks directly to his disciples in a time of distress:

> Do not let your hearts be troubled. Believe in God, believe also in me. In my Father's house there are many dwelling places. . . . I go and prepare a place for you . . . so that where I am, there you may be also. . . . I am the way, and the truth, and the life.

The power of God is greater than the power of death; although the workings of God's power are mysterious. The apostle Paul spoke of death as a transformation, using the image of a seed that is planted in one form and yields—in time—a harvest in a new form. Jesus also spoke of his own death in similar terms, saying that a grain of wheat must die, but when it does, it yields a rich harvest. This is an image that Beth understood during her many years of life.

When a loved one dies, we ask, "Where and how is it possible for us to see the harvest in this event of loss?" Perhaps those who begin to experience the harvest first are those who feel the deepest love and loss. In time, while we must mourn our loss, we may also see how much our lives were enriched by the gift of Beth's life. While it is not easy to surrender Beth into God's care and keeping at this time, we can begin to let go when we thank God that Beth was a part of our lives—as a family member, as a friend—and thank God for our memories of Beth and the time we spent together.

While we cannot fully imagine what the next stage of life is like beyond this one, Beth believed in the promises of the One who said, "I go to prepare a place for you." Because Beth trusted in God's promises, we can be comforted knowing Beth is now in a new place where warm welcomes never end.

Yes, Beth has died; however, Beth's eternal life has just begun. AMEN.

❖   ❖   ❖

In a Heartbeat

Life can be so unpredictable. One day a person is going all out and the next day he or she is gone. This was Frank's story. Frank was the last person anyone would imagine to have heart problems. He lived right, ate right, exercised regularly, and had a lot to live for. Frank was a kind man who was a joy to visit. He had a marvelous sense of humor and enjoyed a practical joke or two. The hours seemed to go like minutes when one was around him.

One afternoon he was sitting on the sofa with family nearby. The heart attack struck without warning; probably he never knew what happened. By the time his body struck the floor, he was gone.

❖   ❖   ❖

Living Life Within the Simplicity of a Smile

Dear friends, we are here to celebrate the life of Frank. Frank was a warm, caring family man. He was a hardworking farmer, a faithful member of the American Legion, and a long-time servant of this community. Frank was blessed with the gifts of simplicity, a warm smile, and an outstretched hand of friendship. Woven in all these attributes was his faith which he lived out every day of his life. Frank was a genuine Christian.

Frank was gifted with the ability to befriend people. It is said that he knew no strangers, and I think that is true. He had a special way of being able to talk gently with folks, to ask questions, and then listen attentively to what the other person had to say. The bench at the mall was a favorite spot of his. Countless times, he sat down next to another farmer and, by the time their wives were finished shopping, Frank knew a good part of the other farmer's life-story. Yes, Frank lived his faith. He reached out to people.

Frank was also blessed with a wonderful sense of humor. He loved to tell jokes or stories. I can still picture how his face would light up, his eyes would twinkle, and his smile would beam as he came to his punchline. Halloween and birthdays were special times for Frank and his family. The family's joy brought joy to many of us. I am sure that most of us here can recall a time in our lives when Frank's smile helped brighten a dreary day. These are precious memories, and we need to keep them dear to us as we let him go to be with God.

Frank was a faithful family man. He used to say that golf and bowling were his hobbies, but his family was his number one interest. He loved organizing outings with his family:

ice-skating parties down by the river, sledding, tobogganing, and much, much more. It gave him great satisfaction to see his children having fun. Yes, there were tough times and sad times. Once, when Frank learned that he was to be the father of twins, he sat down, put his elbows on his knees, rested his tired head in his hands, and said: "Give me strength, Lord, to care for my family." Yet, Frank had a positive outlook on life; he would never surrender to life's dark valleys.

Frank was gifted with practical wisdom. I remember visiting with Frank during my first winter here. Frank sat me down patiently and, in very non-judgmental words, listed the things I needed to have in my car—"just in case." His words were wise and I still follow his advice.

The vitality by which Frank lived life was a constant source of comfort and inspiration to us. His death is made all the more painful because it was so sudden, and because we miss him so. We know that Frank is now with God and at peace; however, that knowledge, while helpful, still leaves an emptiness. In part, that emptiness arises from the questions we all are asking ourselves. "Why Frank?" we ask. "Why now?" No answers present themselves; in the silence, the emptiness remains.

Yet, in time, our emptiness will be filled with what we come to understand as the mystery of love. Love is God's miracle. When we love someone, God has a wonderful way of painting a picture of that person on our hearts. That picture becomes very important. It provides us with a sense of identity, continuity, hope, trust, direction, and meaning for our lives. When a loved one dies, we momentarily lose sight of that picture. We are aware that there is a gaping hole in our hearts. We grieve the loss of our loved one because we are becoming aware of that absence in our lives; however, we also mourn our own inner loss. This is not selfish; this is how God created us. When someone we love passes away, we are hurt. Our pain bears witness to the authenticity of our love.

During the hours, days, months, and even years of grieving, we experience a bewildering mixture of emotions, including denial, anger, bargaining, and despair that leads to acceptance. Often, just when we think we are on top of things, a special smell, sound, food, or date of the year will challenge us, and we are right back to square one. That is OK. That is God's way of helping us learn how to walk again.

Tears have a very special role in this journey of faith. Our tears first say: "Goodbye dear husband, father, and friend." They also have a healing effect. God, in divine wisdom, has a way of using our tears to repaint our loved one's picture on our hearts. However, this time, the picture is drawn of our loved one who is now with God. Over time, our sting of pain will be changed into a deeper appreciation and acceptance of the one we have lost.

Yes, Frank has died; however, Frank's eternal life has just begun. Frank has exchanged the old rugged cross for a crown. AMEN.

❖   ❖   ❖

Midnight's Cry

Jill had a troubled life. Everyone knew that. She had experienced significant personal and professional disappointments. Everyone knew that. She also had a gun—no one knew that.

Jill always presented herself as being tough and positive—ready for that next ride on the bronco. Despite all her setbacks, she helped many in the community face their problems. Late one night, as Jill sat in the dark, she felt overwhelmed by a problem that seemed impossible to deal with—at least for the moment. Jill took the gun out of the drawer. Jill had inspired many people with how she had overcome previous misfortunes in her life. Jill raised the revolver to her head. Jill had a new husband and family—but it seems that she no longer had hope.

❖   ❖   ❖

A Funeral Message at a Time of Suicide
(Based on Psalm 57)

Psalm 57 speaks to us about burdens and risks of life; it reminds us how vulnerable and fragile we humans can be. Yet, rather than falling into despair, the psalmist also reminds us of the amazing grace that comes from God. This comfort can help us in times of need, particularly when we are confronted by unexpected pain.

When the pressures of life beat down on us like the scorching sun, God can provide us with blessed relief. God's presence at such times is like the shade from a tall tree in August heat. When our fears grab hold of us like a hunter's trap, God can be the protective shield we need. When we come to those tough times when we feel we are at rock bottom, God can lift us up to see things differently—from vantage points where even eagles have never soared.

We humans live very private lives. There is so much that we keep to ourselves, and because we do not understand ourselves completely, it is impossible to understand another person fully. No one truly knows another's feelings, hopes, fears, joys, or burdens. Although we do try to understand in some measure, our knowledge is always limited. Just as we all have times of public failure and success, we also have our private obstacles, as well as private triumphs, no one else will really appreciate.

In the past few days, there has been a tragedy. We are left grieving, and we find ourselves asking "Why" and "How?" many times over. Our minds are full of "if onlys." Our hearts want to freeze time and move it backwards. We cannot. Our care and love for Jill is surpassed only by the inner ache in our souls. We long to hear Jill's voice again, but we cannot. Death separates us from Jill, and that knowledge tears at our insides. We are only human, and an experience such as this reminds us that we are painfully limited in what we can do. Death has deprived us of the opportunity to do anything more for Jill, but we can turn to God and to one another to find comfort and hope even in the midst of our loss. Jill is gone. In Jill's passing, we are called to be respectful of others' grieving. There is no room for blame or guilt. In our mutual suffering, let us practice respect, charity, and compassion for one another.

While we will never know what led her to choose a permanent solution to a temporary situation, we do have many wonderful memories of Jill. As difficult as this may be, seek to call those memories to mind. The temptations of "what if" or "if only" will not bring Jill back to us: however, through the wonder of God's amazing grace, God's love is greater than any human act. Jill is with God in a new way, but we, too, are also with God here and now.

This is a hard message to share and to hear. Our ultimate comfort comes in the cross. Through the cross, God understands what we are feeling now in ways that we are not fully aware of. We can also trust that God, the master physician, will heal our broken hearts—if we turn to our Maker.

Jill liked the Fifty-seventh Psalm. It speaks of a comfort that is greater than all our sorrows. Let us turn to God and seek that comfort even as we shed our tears, knowing that the One who provides comfort will hide us in the shadow of God's wings, until the storm passes by. AMEN.

CHAPTER FOUR

After the Funeral

As the fellowship hall begins to empty, there are several general tasks that a clergyperson must do:

(1) See to it that the sanctuary is restored to its normal, non-use state.
(2) Schedule follow-up visits to the bereaved family.
(3) Photocopy any checks that may be given to the clergyperson as a result of services rendered.
(4) Make a note of remuneration in the current year's clergy tax file.
(5) And last, but not least, take some time off to process your feelings.

The funeral marathon can be exhausting. Based upon my personal experiences as well as anecdotes shared by colleagues, a typical funeral will require anywhere from ten to fifteen additional hours of a pastor's professional services. And, as sometimes happens, churches may have to face two or three funerals in a week. This may put a forty-eight hour workload increase on a pastor. Now, consider such a series of events happening (as it often does) during the especially time-intensive seasons of Advent, Lent, Holy Week, and Eastertide.

One need not be a rocket scientist to figure out that such additional pastoral duties may put an overwhelming burden on a pastor and his or her family. This is why it is so terribly important for the pastor to "unplug" and be alone in order to recharge the body and spirit after the funeral. One colleague put it this way: "I worked and worked and then I hit a brick wall. I literally lay on the floor for hours not having the strength to move." Friends, please time to take care of yourselves and mend fences with family members that may have been damaged or strained while you have been caring for the bereaved.

Special Conditions

Wouldn't it be wonderful if everyone loved the pastor? The reality is that a clergyperson will have mixed relationships with his or her parishioners. Sometimes, a clergyperson will relate very well to members of the church; however, on other occasions, the relationships will be tenuous at best. How should a clergyperson behave when dealing with a funeral situation where he or she knows that there has been a history of conflict? [1]

I would be dishonest if I were to say that I had all the answers regarding conflict. When I am aware of a conflicted situation, I am doubly careful to follow the discipline of pastoral care and the other steps of the liturgy to the bereaved. I may well also touch base with a member of my clergy support system for purposes of clarification as well as ventilation of feelings. During this time, I may also increase my time in prayer and make sure I am following proper self-care behaviors (diet, exercise, sleep, and avoiding excess caffeine).

One strategy I have learned to use during such painful experiences is to change my focus of attention and refocus it on something that I can handle. I remember one funeral in particular in which a family and I were on terrible terms. As I visualized having to pastor to that particular family—knowing all the hurtful things they had said and done to me—I shuddered and confessed: "God, I can't do this funeral!" As I prayed for guidance, it occurred to me to focus my attention on something else—in this case the departed. By detaching myself, to a degree, from the history of conflictual encounters with the family, I was able to perform the needed functions for the funeral. I am not saying that I enjoyed the experience; however, at least I was able to implement a strategy that was beneficial to me in an otherwise unbearable situation. Don't let someone else's problem become your undoing.

The second kind of potential minefield involves a family who seeks an outside pastor to officiate at the funeral service. Generally speaking, this occurs when a church's previous pastor cannot resolve his or her separation from the congregation and seeks to reconnect with the congregation by officiating at the service. Most judicatorial officers will discourage such actions because they are viewed as a serious violation of clergy ethics. Most clergy will refrain from such involvements as well.

When my grandmother passed away, I initially contacted my former pastor to perform the services; however, he made it clear that he could not do so ethically. He reminded me that I had a new pastor who should be the one to officiate at my grandmother's funeral. While I was disappointed when my former pastor declined to officiate at the funeral services, I respected his fidelity to his calling—one of the very qualities I admired in him. That was one of his qualities that I appreciated so greatly. This example is not unique. Most clergy will not impose themselves on another pastor's church. Such a practice, as I said before, is generally held to be unseemly, if not outright contemptuous.

Unfortunately, not all clergy honor their respective denomination's code of ethics or follow the guidance of their judicatorial officer in such matters. Occasionally, former pastors will make unilateral decisions and inform the current pastor of their intentions to officiate at the service. This puts the current pastor in a very difficult situation. Generally speaking, the congregation understands that it is the current pastor who is to officiate at all church functions. For another pastor—no matter how beloved by the community—to perform such functions would be seen as a fundamental breach of pastoral ethics. Nonetheless, ultimately, it is far wiser for a clergyperson to graciously and openly facilitate the other pastor's efforts to officiate at the funeral services. The congregation will see that the current pastor is blessed with the important gifts of maturity and flexibility. If such occurrences become habitual, then the local church and the appropriate judicatory officer or board need to take action.

Finally, I need to write a few words about the potential problem of jealous survivors. When a clergyperson directs prolonged pastoral attention to one family, even if such actions are merited, other church members may become jealous. While this may sound childish, I have seen it happen many times. Because of this potentially serious problem, congregational fences have to be mended and ruffled feathers smoothed during the days following the service.

These remarks regarding special conditions cannot cover every possible situation. The one word of advice I can offer is to act in ways that remain true to your calling. I wish you strength and courage for your times of testing.

Pastoral Care

1. Notification of death
   a. Contact family, express condolences, offer brief prayer, and arrange for pastoral visitation.
   b. Preparation for visit:
      i. Make sure home or parsonage and yourself and/or family are secure for an absence of two to three hours.
      ii. Put church directory and map in the car along with a book of prayer and Bible.
      iii. Contact designated person who coordinates the notification of church family about the death and tell that person where you will be for the next few hours. Also, the following persons should be notified:
         (1) Secretary
         (2) Custodian
         (3) Groundskeeper
         (4) P/S sound technician
2. Bereavement visitation
   a. Initial Contact with the bereaved family:
      i. Express condolences.
      ii. Learn the names of the parties present at the home.
   b. Triage care

    i. Quickly determine the needs of the family.

    ii. Identify problems that need to be dealt with immediately.

c. Attentive listening:

    i. Ascertain stability of situation.

    ii. Give permission for the bereaved to ventilate the experience.

    iii. Provide appropriate empathetic presence.

    iv. Identify emotional support system for the bereaved.

d. Closure:

    i. Express condolences again.

    ii. Have a prayer (brief).

    iii. Provide business card and invite the bereaved to contact you when they are ready.

    iv. Exit

Appendix B

Funeral Planning Guide

Name: _____

Date of service: _____

Time of service: _____

Location of service: _____

Location of committal service: _____

Musicians/music: _____

_____

Married to: _____ on _____, __
at _____ .

Lived at: 1. _____
2. _____
3. _____

Born: _____

Went to school at: _____

_____

_____

Offspring: 1. _____
2._____
3._____

Career life: 1. _____
2. _____
3. _____

Interests in life: 1. _____
2. _____
3. _____

Hobbies: 1. _____
2. _____
3. _____

Happy memories of:
1. _____
_____
2. _____
_____
3. _____
_____
4. _____
_____
5. _____
_____

Congregational hymns: (optional)
1. _____
2. _____

Hymn suggestions

"My Hope Is Built
 on Nothing Less"
"Blessed Assurance"
"How Great Thou Art"

"Abide with Me"
"Forward Through the Ages"
"Great Is Thy Faithfulness"
"For All the Saints"

"Blessed Be the Tie   "How Firm a Foundation"
   That Binds"   "In the Garden"
"A Mighty Fortress   "Amazing Grace"
Is Our God"

Favorite scripture passages or poems:

1. _____

2. _____

3. _____

4. _____

5. _____

Suggested scriptures: Old Testament

Job 19:25-27 (My redeemer lives)
Psalm 23 (Shepherding)
Psalm 27:7-14 (Lament: wait on the Lord)
Psalm 42:1-5 (My soul pants for God)
Psalm 46 (God: Refuge and strength)
Psalm 91 (On eagles' wings)
Psalm 121 (Look to the hills)
Psalm 139:1-18, 23-24 (God knows us)
Ecclesiastes 3:1-8 (Seasons)
Isaiah 25:6-9 (God swallows up death)
Isaiah 61:1-3 (Spirit of the Lord is upon me)
Lamentations 3:22-26, 31-33 (Great is thy faithfulness)
Ezekiel 37:1-10 (Dry bones)

New Testament

Matthew 5:3-10 (Beatitudes)
Matthew 11:28-30 (Giving rest)
Luke 23:33, 39-43 (Robber forgiven)
John 6:37-40 (Believing/Raising)
John 11:17-27 (Lazarus)
John 12:24-26 (Honoring my servants)
John 14:1-3, 18-19, 25-27 (Many rooms)
Romans 8:31-39 (God is for us)
1 Corinthians 13 (Love)
1 Corinthians 15:12-30, 35-50 (Resurrection)

2 Corinthians 4:16-18 (Inner person renewed)
2 Corinthians 5:1-5 (Having a building of grace)
Ephesians 3:14-21 (Rooted and grounded in love)
1 Thessalonians 4:13-18 (Those who are asleep)
Revelation 21:1-6 (A new Jerusalem)

Special needs: 1. _____

2._____

Number of people expected to be at the funeral service:

Review what will happen on the day of the funeral. Ask if the family would find it helpful for the pastor to attend the public viewing of the departed.

Pray for the family.

Leading Worship

1. Clergy walkthrough—done well before the anticipated arrival of the departed's family.
   a. Check sanctuary:
      i. Put service file on pulpit with sermon inside.
      ii. Mark Bible for designated reading.
      iii. Check lights, fans, furnace, a/c.
      iv. Put glass of water on pulpit.
      v. Check doors and windows.
   b. Check kitchen and fellowship hall:
      i. Check the status of beverage and meal preparation.
      ii. Thank the workers for their efforts.
      iii. Ask if the workers have any questions or have any specific needs.
   c. Check grounds:
      i. Outside doors.
      ii. Chairs for family prayer service.
      iii. Sidewalks.
      iv. Parking lot.
2. Coordinating with funeral service principal parties.
   a. Funeral director:
      i. Give service outline.
         (1) Review service choreography.
         (2) Time check.
      ii. Talk to organist.

          (1) Give service outline.

          (2) Review service choreography.

          (3) Check to see if there are any specific needs.

          (4) Time check.

       iii. Check with soloist(s):

          (1) Give service outline.

          (2) Review service choreography.

          (3) Check to see if there are any specific needs.

          (4) Time check.

3. Final worship preparations.
   a. Complete paperwork:
      i. Pastor's card to the bereaved family.
      ii. Official recording of funeral service in pastor's record book.
      iii. Robe/proper attire.
      iv. Check oneself in the mirror.
      v. Pause to pray.
4. Visit with the bereaved family.
   a. Greet family.
   b. Find out if there are any last-minute instructions or announcements that need to be made.
5. Funeral service/Committal service (see sample funeral services).
6. Consolation meal.
   a. Say grace.
   b. Direct the people to gather depending on the manner in which food will be served.
   c. Give the bereaved family the pastor's card and devotional.
   d. Eat with the bereaved family (if requested).
   e. Excuse oneself after saying goodbye to the family.

Sample Funeral Service for a Man

Funeral Service of: _____

Date: _____

Location: _____

Prepared by: _____

Prelude

Welcoming Words

O God, you are our Good Shepherd. You lead us in ways of nurture and renewal in order that we may live uprightly to your glory. Even in times of testing, your rod and staff are a comforting presence to us. As we surrender our lives to you again even in this most trying time of the dark valley, we hold on to your promise that your goodness and mercy shall be with us all the days of our lives and that our hearts may dwell with you everyday—even as we gather to pay our final respects to the life of _____. AMEN.

Words of Purpose

Friends, this is God's dwelling place. We are here under the shelter of God's grace to say goodbye to _____ as we surrender him to God's eternal care. At this holy time, God grants us permission to open our hearts, shed our tears, and acknowledge our pain and emptiness even as we draw strength from the promises of God for our lives. While we know that all of us are made out of dust and will one day return to dust, we also believe that through the resurrection of Christ, death's sting has been healed with the gift of eternal life with God. Friends, we are humbly a people of God. Let us draw strength from one another as we lament our mutual loss.

Prayer of Invocation

O God, you have searched us and known us. You are familiar with all our ways. Such knowledge is too wonderful for us. Even in the darkness of this moment, when we open to you our hearts filled with anguish as we remember the life of your faithful servant and dread the prospect of separation that death brings, you are here with us. Grant us, O Lord, a degree of your understanding and peace as you lead us always in your ways. AMEN.

Obituary and Reading of Scripture

Message

Pastoral Prayer and Lord's Prayer

O Lord of comfort and compassion, the family and friends of your faithful servant _____ offer heartfelt thoughts of gratitude for his life now that he has journeyed from this world and his spirit lives now in your care and keeping. Although it is hard to say goodbye to _____, because we love him, we also rejoice that he has become a new creation and we must release our grasp that he may celebrate his new life with you, O God. Meet us here, O Lord, and bind our wounded hearts with your love and healing power. Bless all who loved _____ as they remember him today and as they continue their lives in the days to come. May they find assurance that you are with them as you are also with _____ [1]. Join me in saying the Lord's Prayer.

Announcements

(References to committal service and consolation meal may be made here.)

Final Thanksgiving for the Departed

O Good Shepherd, receive _____ into your eternal fold with love and tenderness. We offer you thanks for his life. Grant peace as he joins the blessed cloud of witnesses that have gone before us.

Benediction

Now may God bless you and keep you. May God's face shine upon and be gracious to you. May God look upon you with kindness and grant each one of you peace. AMEN.

Recessional Hymn or Music

Sample Funeral Service for a Woman

Funeral Service of: _____

Date: _____

Location: _____

Prepared by: _____

Prelude

Welcoming Words

O God, you are our Good Shepherd. You lead us in ways of nurture and renewal in order that we may live uprightly to your glory. Even in times of testing, your rod and staff are a comforting presence to us. As we surrender our lives to you again, even in this most trying time of the dark valley, we hold on to your promise that your goodness and mercy shall be with us all the days of our lives and that our hearts may dwell with you every day—even as we gather to pay our final respects to the life of _____. AMEN.

Words of Purpose

Friends, this is God's dwelling place. We are here under the shelter of God's grace to say goodbye to _____ as we surrender her to God's eternal care. At this holy time, God grants us permission to open our hearts, shed our tears, and acknowledge our pain and emptiness even as we draw strength from the promises of God for our lives. While we know that all of us are made out of dust and will one day return to dust, we also believe that through the resurrection of Christ, death's sting has been healed with the gift of eternal life with God. Friends, we are humbly a people of God. Let us draw strength from one another as we lament our mutual loss.

Prayer of Invocation

O God, you have searched us and known us. You are familiar with all our ways. Such knowledge is too wonderful for us. Even in the darkness of this moment, when we open to you our hearts filled with anguish as we remember the life of your faithful servant and dread the prospect of separation that death brings, you are here with us. Grant us, O Lord, a degree of your understanding and peace as you lead us always in your ways. AMEN.

Obituary and Reading of Scripture

Message

Pastoral Prayer and Lord's Prayer

O Lord of comfort and compassion, the family and friends of your faithful servant _____ offer heartfelt thoughts of gratitude for her life now that she has journeyed from this world and her spirit lives now in your care and keeping. Although it is hard to say goodbye to _____, because we love her, we also rejoice that she has become a new creation and we must release our grasp that she may celebrate her new life with you, O God. Meet us here, O Lord, and bind our wounded hearts with your love and healing power. Bless all who loved _____ as they remember her today and as they continue their lives in the days to come. May they find assurance that you are with them as you are also with _____.[1] Join me in saying the Lord's Prayer.

71

Announcements

(References to committal service and consolation meal may be made here.)

Final Thanksgiving for the Departed

O Good Shepherd, receive _____ into your eternal fold with love and tenderness. We offer you thanks for her life. Grant peace as she joins the blessed cloud of witnesses that have gone before us.

Benediction

Now may God bless you and keep you. May God's face shine upon and be gracious to you. May God look upon you with kindness and grant each one of you peace. AMEN.

Recessional Hymn or Music

Sample Funeral Service Outline

Funeral Service of: _____

Date: _____

Location: _____

Prepared by: _____

Prelude

Welcoming Words

Words of Purpose

Prayer of Invocation

Obituary and Reading of Scripture

Message

Pastoral Prayer and Lord's Prayer

Announcements
(References to committal service and consolation meal may be made here.)

Final Thanksgiving for the Departed

Benediction

Recessional Hymn or Music (optional)

Sample Committal Service

Opening words

We gather here for the time of committal.

Scripture (Isaiah 40:31)

> But those who wait for the Lord shall renew their
> strength,
>   they shall mount up with wings like eagles,
> they shall run and not be weary,
>   they shall walk and not faint.

Statement of Committal

We commit, O merciful God, to your eternal care the remains of _____ to the earth, trusting in your providential mercy.

Prayer

Just as doubting Thomas came to believe in the resurrection, help us also understand the mystery of eternal life you promise us. Be a source of comfort and direction to us. Uphold us in all our daily efforts so that we may uplift your holy name and righteous ways. AMEN.

Benediction

Go now in peace, ever mindful of what you have witnessed here today. Blessed are those who mourn, for they shall be comforted. AMEN.

NOTES

1. The Phone Rings

1. I do not want to give the false impression that the grief process and grief work are insignificant matters. Elisabeth Kübler-Ross's classic work, *On Death and Dying*, should be required reading for all seminarians. Without such tools, clergy pastoral care is difficult; however, the media has tended to oversimplify and trivialize Kübler-Ross's groundbreaking work.

2. This is important! People come to funerals dressed as if they were attending a regular church service; however, they forget about the possibility of an outdoor committal service. I have seen people gather for a committal service wearing only their dress clothes in sub-zero weather. One funeral is enough; don't encourage additional funerals by having people not dress for the elements! This means that before a clergyperson gets into the hearse for the ride to the cemetery, he or she also needs to put the necessary winter wraps, sunglasses, gloves, and snowboots into the hearse. Remember, clergy can get sick too!

3. For a helpful discussion about the topic of presentation see Rosemary Marshall Balsam and Alan Balsam, *Becoming a Psychotherapist* (Chicago: The University of Chicago Press, 1984), 39.

4. For those who have not received such training, please see Allen E. Ivey, *Intentional Interviewing and Counseling* (Monterey: Brooks/Cole, 1983). This work provides a step-by-step guide for training of counselor to do intentional interviews.

5. Of course, this comment is modified when death strikes the pastor's family. In that case, I would recommend that the pastor from a sister church officiate at the service as well as provide the normal pastoral care. Denominations vary on this question. In some, judicatorial representatives may participate or even officiate at the service.

6. For a helpful discussion on how a family comes to an "updated" understanding of itself, see Virginia Satir, *The New Peoplemaking* (Mountainview: Science and Behavior Books, 1988), 36-37.

7. The use of the Lord's Prayer is very powerful. Besides the sacred understandings associated with the prayer, it is a prayer that a good number of people know and tend to be comfortable praying in unison. The prayer also provides the bereaved with a sense of control and familiarity amidst very chaotic and strange times. Finally, when no further words can be said, many see this prayer as a liturgical benediction that announces closure to the community.

8. On occasion, the use of poetry, especially by grandchildren, may become counterproductive. It can underscore a competitive game of "I loved Grandma or Grandpa the most and I was Grandpa's or Grandma's favorite." I have tactfully redirected such statements so that they are understood to represent the entire family, not only one person speaking or misspeaking out of personal pain.

9. Robert Frost, "Departmental", *Complete Poems of Robert Frost 1949*, (New York: Henry Holt, 1949), 373.

2. Preparing for the Funeral Sermon

1. A pastor I know had to be very careful about the remarks he made at one funeral. Apparently, the departed had died in the very act of committing adultery. The pastor had to be very careful about how he characterized the departed's ability to express caring to those he met!

2. For further substantiation of this point, see the following works: Nancy Tuckerman and Nancy Dunnan, *The Amy Vanderbilt Complete Book of Etiquette* (New York: Doubleday, 1995), 445; and Elizabeth Post, *Emily Post's Etiquette*, 15th ed. (New York: HarperCollins, 1992), 555.

4. After the Funeral

1. There are times when a clergyperson is unaware of hurt feelings, too. This makes pastoring very challenging. One never really knows how one is doing with another person. This is precisely what makes the art of marriage, of family life, and of church life so frustrating and yet potentially so rewarding.

Appendix D

1. By The Reverend Dr. Allene M. Parker. Used by permission.

Appendix E

1. By The Reverend Dr. Allene M. Parker. Used by permission.